My book of poems

Miss Ratul Banerjee

 pencil

ISBN 978-93-5610-602-4
© miss ratul banerjee 2022
Published in India 2022 by Pencil

A brand of
One Point Six Technologies Pvt. Ltd.
123, Building J2, Shram Seva Premises,
Wadala Truck Terminal, Wadala (E)
Mumbai 400037, Maharashtra, INDIA
E connect@thepencilapp.com
W www.thepencilapp.com

DISCLAIMER: *The opinions expressed in this book are those of the authors and do not purport to reflect the views of the Publisher.*

Author biography

hi i am miss ratul banerjee and i have a distinct penchant for writing poems and doing acrylic artwork . i   am a BSC physics honours graduate   from   Calcutta University   and pursued computer   education . my paintings can be   seen in fineartamerica.com website
my   book aims to capture the quiet reflective moments that come back again   softly dancing along the memory strings be it sun rise be it the moon light enigma , but that i   truly revel in these recollections , like a dream ..... within a dream ......

CONTENTS

reiterations

there i was .... once upon a while
present finds it just a faded obscure strip of memory with
wings to fly
unrestricted through the tunnels, corridors of a dormant
mind yet not awakened by any trigger
and i still wish i was there ....
every while i close the eyes in rest
a bleak perchance sensing feeling it , that abstraction
shrouded in mystery coming before my eyes as a
mysterious bird in flight , flapping the stretched wings
it wants to communicate with me , perhaps in a different
sign language unknown to me
in the slightest anticipation i understand or decipher its
code
.... sometimes , there's just a flicker of strong light
before the eyes , then seeing in the flash light beautiful
picturesque scenes of glacial lakes underneath sprawling
meadows , lofty mountains
still following the thought bird as it discreetly flies over a
beautiful log cabin situated high up on the meadows
the ecstasy the exhilarating moment as if paradise is a
stone's throw away
.... see , my life's sad , unfortunate
and i still believe if i can start life again
albeit risks beckon i may not be living any longer

.... in case if i die .... the gates of paradise shall open for me
.... the transcendence journeying of the soul past the spatial frontiers , directed by and into the light fields
till finding happiness again in a new place a different time
....

the darkest dark

If I am the darkest dark
The annihilation of every Lacuna of light
Then why am I so particular or unique
In my chosen or accepted verdict of a light bereft world
In my eyes that light and dark follow in intrepid footsteps
The light cannot manifest without a dark background
Because there is steadfast light in the world that's why darkness gets a chance to prove itself or exemplify
What's the nature inherent attribute in the universe
The black holes or cold or frozen energy hot spots that absorb light
Else the tremendous powered quantized light particles as energy waves through thermonuclear reactions in the sun and millions of solar systems
But the fact remains universe is devoid of inherent light as it is devoid of absolute darkness
The energy balance equation the entropy of universe is never a positive
Whence death encountered on me
Wondering if this is the end
But there's indistinct evidence to support in transcendence and after death experience
The unvanquished meta entity the soul manifested as the orb in its transcendence journey through the cosmos the blurry tunnels or connector between a million planets stars

and like wise
No end is sufficient no inception was enough justified
Where I started on earth in fact my root cause origin was
from the universe the massive infinite Ness
Where I will die by the invincible law of universe only to
merge again in the primordial energy fields
Time is meaningless there space is redundant there

no need

My life is sad
And I have a subtle feeling that I shall perish inevitably
earlier
Well things I wanted to accomplish
Places that I wanted to visit ......
Now that dreams are already dead
With perhaps little chances of reviving
Unhappiness or sadness a futile lament
And like the fall of a thousand detached leaves from trees
I shall perhaps depart from earth home unconditionally
and with unattached strings
Whence love lost friend less knew no sympathy even from
uncaring parents
A destiny dependent life
....
A sultry night fall the still air the deafening silence
Before falling asleep and spending some time In quiet
contemplation
A unheard sigh of morose I utter that gets lost in
translation
Nobody listens everybody pretends
.... today that I want whole heartedly to get this life I lead
ended
Praying for nothing but the end
If that could initiate a new lease of lost chances amidst

sadness that has weighed me down
The silence retorts back ......
Darkness intensified
Looking out of the window gazing at the moon light
spectacle
....
The lament : somehow my parents needed me
Now they need me no longer ....

albeit

Will you remember me
Even after I am gone
Obliterated from mortal life
No more
Will you remember me
Albeit I exist no longer
And the leaves still fall off from dead twigs
And the wind still blows over my grave in the cemetery
The withered flower petals land astray on the concrete
Will you remember me
Be it fall be it the spring harmony
Be it the regale winter come
And I live no more
Will you remember me
On the perfect dawn breaking
As the resplendent dew drops gather on grass blades
On the divine moonlit nights
As a solitary kayak drifts on the ebbs and tides
Of the river named destiny
Will you remember me
Lest I have died
Did I really ?
The imperceptible voice of nature .tells
Me a different story
It speaks about my existence or presence

Felt in every subtle touch of nature
Will you remember me
In the gold hues in autumn come
The kans grass sways in the breeze
Lest I am gone forever ....
And I can't love you any longer
Albeit
Will you remember me even then

where dreams melt

where dreams will find an answer one day
albeit i exist no more
where the rivers drain into the oceans
and the oceans bleed into the endless magnitude of skies
a rare moment at a fag day;s end
the trace of golden light left on the endless waters
like a virtual pathway or connector to paradise and beyond
and who am i?
not of this world though
an unrequited spirit
like a free entity , drifting off and above the seas the lands
to an unknown destination
where no man has intrepid so far
the sunset come , as for a brief spell
the transient light and exposes the virtual paths
across the seas stretching into the void
in ever quest of unending peace
.... did i find it
and as if in response to my passive query
the sea bird flies high up above the gold and crimson
rimmed clouds
until oblivion
a point of extremes
of no return , and forever forgetfulness

river of tears

The river of forever tears flow by in the breaking moment
of the dawn
albeit the sun rise and the burst of light in the ambient sky
still ….. like a dirge, have I died ?
The birds fly into the endless expanse
dark shadows throng in the subdued light , the riverside
no man in vicinity , but a solitary boat moored to the
shores
even in the shadows of void, perhaps embedded in the
depths
lies a hidden story as the dead or lost names are called back
again
and even if I am to believe that I exist no more …….
there's a contradiction …….. where the energy spectrum
in the sky, the lands tell a different story
the winds set trees sway, leaves fall and the tiny wavelets
form on the water surface
there's somewhat a lingering sadness in the overall theme
reflective, why my life's a failed try , sadness
if I am to believe in after death transcendence
have I already embarked on the mission ?
don't look out for me in the conventional hours
look out for me at this juncture, the awakening of just
another day
with the primordial sunrise , with the accumulating fog on

the river side
I shall come …. slowly, intrepid tip toeing past the fastened doors of the landscape
no one notices, no one knows lest
the one exception in the solitary mysterious boat by the riverside
waiting there for endless, timeless enigmatic times
……….. the last passenger maybe is the spirit in I …….
a strange sad tale of longing and expectations, in anticipation
sadly lost out to the eternal waves in spaces

the orphan

The orphan soul
Unsung in life mostly
Unloved by all
Even parents
That she grew up like a careless vegetation growth amidst a
bunch of carefully pruned flower primes
Loathed by all
No reasons suffice
Neglected in life
Even ignored in death
Whence her grave after demise is still unattended and
uncatered
A thick growth of ferns and thorny trees
Whilst dust and dirt blown in the uprising wind
A cold night a pale moon floats by
A night bird suddenly flies out in rendezvous
The veil of mist in the ambience
Murky outlines and the black hound barks resonate in the
stark void nothingness
The cemetery gate man strolls by nonchalantly
Forgets or purposefully enough doesn't wait by this
neglected grave
A swarm of clumsy insects crawl by unfettered along the
marshy outlines
Rise of the eerie wind a fall in the pattern

The pause thereafter a spell of deafening silence
Even in the shadows even in death
Why
No matter why
.... The unexplained sad story of an orphan soul

the song out of time

I loved you and I lost you
Through spanning the several lapses of past life
Now a obscure mark rising from the worn out pages of my
memory scrap book
Every time in restful disposition and I think about
Slowly silently yielding in to the realm of dreaming
A meta physical world that carry me far and wide
Overriding my conscious mind even
Scaling mountain highs pervading the barriers of rivers and
rocky terrains
A mist rises from the abyss of murky past life
My overwhelming moment in ecstasy as I can indistinct see
you again
Standing over that cliff at a distance
Whilst ecstatic I want to follow you
Reaching out to you ......
Lest the mist intensifies a foggy cloud
A blurred mind a one time beautiful journeying only to
meet you only to be lost again

....
I will see you again
You 're never really gone
I can feel you walk beside me
In my darkest hour or despair in my blithe

I keep telling myself
I will see you again

sad tears

The unconditionally black child
I
Daughter of a lesser God
Or a partial different super power in the indelible
That ignored me right since inception
Born with mental scars and destined to be a loser
In life that's an always gloomy and tough road journey for
me
I have no friends
I have no well wishers
My eyes bleed in unseen tears of forever sadness
Fell down many times
And now the fall is an endless fathomless pit
From where I cannot rise
I know no love in my sad life
I know not to express my love if any for anybody
Mistakes I did unknowingly
And the cruel judgment of destiny
The penalty price is too heavy
Now ......
On the bleak shores of a foggy riverside
Seeing empty minded a boat or two ply on the waters
My eyes moisten in unknown tears of forever morose
The boatman didn't take me
If

I could sail away to the far fields of fortune
Now .....
That's gone forever
A futile wait for nothing
A wasted life
And sad tears won't stop falling

sadness

Autumn come the soft winds blow
Over the golden crops in fields
The spotless skies where drifts by
A array of non nimbus clouds
A wild duck or two wade unfettered in the sluggish waters
of still pond
The kans grass sway non chalant by the riverside
No more rains the lush green of landscape
Finds a subtle replacement in prosaic shades of brown or
raw sienna burnt amber
The description adhered to a typical rustic scene of Bengal
Whilst the dhakìs at a distance beat their drums and play
the clarionet
A welcoming tune sung in reverence of the goddess Durga
Autumn come Durga Puja knocks at the invisible door of
the rustic landscape
Be it early morning be it dusk fall
And the skies in every instant beaming in the festive hues
as if reflected in the skies
The gentle winds time and again
The ripples set amidst the flow of river waters
A black swan lifts off into the sunset sky
A translucent fog emerges In the ambience
All the remnant colours in the skies the lands now mingle
in blend

A different feel still beatitude even in the rare the
unknown flavour
My heart still catches on with the festive spirit
As the dhakis still sound their drums and the reverberating
sound at a distance
Lest darkness now reigns in the sunset after light
And lesser choices left than walk home even if unwillingly
Following the rustic meandering lanes cutting through the
fields
Still hearing indistinct the sound of drums and the
clarionet
.... home reached night falls
Still anticipating for the next dawn come
Sensing the dew drops accumulate on grass blades
And then again going outside to the riverside
Seeing the kans grass sway in the breeze
And the wild ducks swim unfettered in the waters

....

Autumn come
Am I indeed happy
Else the feel of bless lingers somewhere I do not know
Surpassing this life beyond backtracking to past life
regressive travel
...... if could retrace following the strange music of the flute
In or out of sync with the festive mood

home beyond

my mind is imprisoned , trapped yet by the unforeseen
the unconditional things, the impeding sadness, sorrow
alone in a vast empty colossus, still in quest of thrill and
adventure
where definitely the mind is not bogged down by fear and
apprehension
should I disclose frankly that I not a chip of the old block
the rare , the exception that I am and will be throughout
this life's twists and turns, notwithstanding any thing ,
anybody
my inherent identity or orientation is that I am a lesbian
a lesser known introvert , who has no friends,
still seeks and finds solace in the finer nature elements
every time, I go to the green meadows nearness to my
place
in the squashy sunfilled days, and the air gusts set cumulus
clouds drifting
the skies render a gray hue , whilst a light drizzle
with the sunshine only to proliferate and manifest as a
splendid rainbow effect in the heavens
at this moment, there's an exhilarating unexplained ecstasy
in me
forgetting the drudgery awhile, and aspiring yet to run wild
like the wild horses of the barn, in the background of
picturesque valleys and cerulean skies

tell me, I believe god or the omnipresent is a gender-less abstraction
more in the lines of being a brilliant trans gendered identity, one massive artist inspiration , one great poet , the connoiseur of fine arts, creativity and talent, the patron of the beautiful
I want to go where the Zephyr really originates from
that extreme end of the skies , tracking the black bird's trajectory
I want to drift on and on, in the high weather and the ebbs and the ultimate rest ? Else a new start on a different journeying past the skies higher and higher until the point of oblivion or forgetfulness
death …..? yes, mortal end but I still exist
else where above the clouds in the skies , home beyond

the powered belief

Winter immortal songs coming back again and again
even after the seasonal progression
reminiscence about the lost , cast away and forgotten
dreams
the implicit sadness , an unknown feel in the atmosphere
before sun sets and the accumulating fog
leaves blurry outlines of the helios and a swarm of cranes
fly high up above the glacial lakes
reflective moments, contemplating if in the alarmingly high
birds cries
is captured the cherished but lost out dreams ,if could be
re-lived
nonetheless, what is lost is forever
maybe the congregating sorrow of missing out something,
someone, somewhere
in the background of a beautiful picturesque winter scenes
just augments and proliferates the wild spirit latent in every
soul
I am born free ….. just that inhibitions and societal
impediments matter
lest the awakening of my real self , the wild spirit as sacred
and pure like the yeha noha
maybe gives me impetus to move on and on
albeit no more bodily, but the soul traversal ……
I can almost see and feel the beautiful aurora borealis lights

in the sunset skies
I can now almost feel the vibrations and weak signals
conveyed by the flight of arid leaves falling off in the air
drag
they want to communicate with me , …..
just that a time difference even if subtle
and the wilderness, the ethnic earth spirit is already in me
no harm will befall me any time, any where, any more …..

cosmic citizen

In my eyes death not the end
But the initiation to the potential life after death
Where one day I will die by the natural law
Lest at the sunset hour my air plane comes
Swooning past the sky canopy of cosmic dust and inter
galactic matter
And here I go embarking in grace on the air plane
Lifting off the earth station
Flying high and higher crossing the cover of clouds
Into the colossus of cerulean skies higher higher
Until the point of oblivion
Earth address becomes a distant and faded reminiscence
And I or the very absence of the mortal self that once was
Slowly definitely on the way to becoming a cosmic citizen

once awhile

Once in a year , a fantastic exhilarating moment reckons
one breath taking instant in heaven calls home from
beyond perception,
in that winter advents in style, regale a dance, looking
bespectacled
at the array of incessant snow fall, everywhere beautiful in
white
the place where I live, a distant off beat place faraway from
the madding crowds and into the endless expanse of
woods and forests
laden with towering pine and firs , the remnant arid leaves
have already given way ,
and now whatever remains adorns in bejeweled white glory
, ice flanked
and the ice covered rustic lanes running through this vast
expanse
the half frozen river waters , where throngs a flight of
migratory birds
now its well past rolling deep into the evening with a
sunken helios
an ethereal glow lingers in the last drops of radiant
sunbeams
a medley of shadows and interspersing light on the forest
ground
on the way through nameless roads running through

unknown corners of this land
exploring rare cracks and crevices in woods , seeing
suddenly a flash of bright colors as a multi hued exotic bird
flies from tree to trees
well, dusk fall and the cold north winds set shivers
a creepy fog , a translucent settings in this outdoors
leaving space for more bewilderment , ethereal light
whatever sparse cottages on the roadside, the roof is ice
covered
and my meager foot prints left on the ice flanked roads
covering yet another distance , walking for nameless yards
undirected a drift almost like the cold north winds
letting go of every inhibition and worries, even if no longer
happiness
still inexplicably seeing through and into a new meaning of
living
this time only for myself and me alone …….

the sadness

Here I am, standing still for nameless times and infinite
ages
the random high winds and the escalated storm could not
destroy my existence
I have withstand the ravages of the killer element the much
loathed rain
as I have , like the dark stature of a dark pagan woman
welcomed in unknown blithe and unfelt ecstasy
the beautiful winter , as the land is draped in gleaming
white ice magic
and the symmetrical ice flakes fall listless for endless time
lapses
here I stand, the dark outlines of a leaf-bereft giant tree ,
silhouetted in the background of the blazing sunlight and
the plangent moonlight
don't underestimate my inner hidden potential
I can summon and call the dark elusive forces of a
forbidden outer worldly existence
every while the mighty winds sway in encircled fringes
about me
that's when I sound , the subdued or suppressed cries and
sobs speaking in an inexplicit way , about my secret wiccan
and dark powers
I cry ….. and somewhere nearby in the woods
a dead twig breaks , a wooden rupture sounds

whilst night fall , and the chiropteran creatures fly out of the hideouts in frenzied myriad pathways
my dark potential, proclaims me as the tree of death ……
beware ….. don't step near me , I am only bound to destroy or demolish every creature
only come to me as a sacrifice or bait,
the sacrifice you are offering yourself at my powered pedestal
be the least afraid, I shall entwine you in the armor of death like a giant spider discreetly alerted weaving it's intricate cobwebs
the tree of death I am, nocturnal hours , the sky alight in stars and the pale moon light
here I am, here I will indeed remain , a still-life for the rest of the years , time after time ……
I once sought a friend amidst the resplendent leaves , but the fly leaf departed away in the air drift ……
so, I the bereaved soul, cries unheard tears, unseen and unfelt by all
…… a sad story of love lost …. lingering in the shadows of a timeless enigma ,powered existence, none can understand …… and the sad tears won't stop falling

unending sadness

The orphan soul or conscience within a sad self retorts out
in dismay
Why my life is this sadness
A perennial river of tears
That nothing nobody no circumstance can suffice
Why am I destined or indirectly cursed by destiny to be a
loser
Whence I had almost every thing beside me
Some wealth some assets yes some talents and skills yes
Then why
The last train whizzes off at break neck speed to the great
outdoors
A wheel chaired guy that's me waits on the balcony of my
old home
Gazing empty minded at the run away train
It did not take me ....
A crescendo of leaves fall off in the rising wind
A sad soul I stretched out her meagre hand to hold the fly
leaf
Lest it slipped away ....
Unending tears and the tear drops won't stop falling

i don't want the world to save me

An endless expanse... golden hue desert sands
A vast colossal sea of sands since nameless ages
Surpassing time and space
Ethereal, magical even in the bright day light
When a brilliant Helios transits thro' the azure skies
Sunset, in the after light... a short lived moment
Cause sooner to transit into nocturnal haze
When starry heavens, crescent moon
No demarcating borderline between this endless sea of sands and the skies
The Syrian desert, where sands of time flows past the abyss or ridges of space
Endless spectacle, magnificent and alluringly beautiful
These desert of Syria share their borders with the blessed kingdom Jordan and the Arabian Peninsula
Here time is a static and history.....nomads and Bedouins stays there
The Iraq War did enough to rip apart this beautiful Nature scape
As the military tanks would patrol down the yellow desert sands
Rummaging the nomads' tents and homes, of the villagers and land mines
Amputated limbs, as the innocent children too fall a victim
Syrian deserts then..... into a plenitude carcass... bloody

battle grounds
.... slowly, silently..... limping back to normalcy once again
But the wounds... the aftermath of war.... take time to heal
That's Zebba, the little nomad girl whose house is amidst these Syrian desert sands
She lost her limbs.... ugly warfare claimed it..... all gave some
And some unconditionally gave all.... the galore of war
The dark curtains of the nightfall as it ushers in, over this colossal landscape
A starry eyed Zebba stands atop the sand dunes, a vacant look in her eyes
Looking at the star fields above her head and she is contemplative as she mutters silently
 " I don't want the world to save me
Cause I don't think that they'd understand
When everything's meant to be broken
I just want you to know who I am "

silk routes of dead dreams

A never ending saga
The endless bohemian spirit
A vagabond soul journeying and scaling
Through a stunningly beautiful mountainous terrain
Must I rest for infinite time on the lofty cliffs
Weaving carefully the long lost threads or memory strings
Day and night whilst the sunlight and the moon beams
Adding a niche to this creative instinct
Must I live in the mountain regions as long as I live
Where death besets
The faded perceptibility or a blurry feeling
That I am still there
Where every time the leaf fall initiated in the Zephyr
I am still there ..... as a faint vibration of rustic earth
Where every time the translucent fog covers the mystic
lands
I am still there like a miniature particle of the air stream
The picturesque landscape and the brook gushes along
It's riverine journey past many a wood a creek or a crevice
I am still there felt as a intangible presence
Amidst the pebbles lacing the water shores

My death was not the ultimate end
Larger than life here I am
Still weaving the silk routes of dead dreams

lost out

lost winter , beautiful in white
enriched woods sparkling and beautiful even in the
stark emptiness and void, depths of nothingness
scarce footsteps tread the rustic lanes
but every chances of the rare humanoids
elf , fairy and the goblin yet walking with bemused ecstasy
early morning advent finds smoggy skies
fog filled woods,a thin translucent film of wet vapor in the
atmosphere
a liquefied effect rendering amidst the forests
as if the towering trees are melting down , slowly
moisture drooping from the last remnants of arid leaves
an unknown unexplored world beckons from beyond
a no man's land, the woods, still it's the coveted haven
for the scarcely visible humanoids …………...
have you ever seen a Troll or a clumsy goblin?
No , I haven't but the sixth sense or intuitive self
makes me feel every time I go to the woods
even in the shadows, these little creatures of a different
world are yet there
just that I am falling behind or falling out of step
to keep in pace with little men ………...

the mask

If I wear a mask
Would you see through the mask
To see the real self I am
Behind the lifeless parchment like mask
Peeling it off like onion scales
The rare sight of a still innocent face
Drooping singed eyelids that carefully
Cover the popped out green eyes
That like a bewildered child
Staring bemused at the world
But let me tell you
I am not simple
Living through a duality existence
Personality disorder I am
Both innocent as a child
And profane as a witch
Every dark hour I stand beside the mirror
Hanging on the wall then carefully pull apart the mask
Mirror mirror tell the truth
In the fallen light after dusk fall
Waiting eagerly to find an answer
But what I feel is a soundness echo
Of several lost whims once dreamt of
Mirror mirror tell the truth
No response that way still the responsive medium

Hasn't yet died down.
Before night falls in the fading light
The only communicativeness between me
And the mirror past the glass interface